Inside Animals

Frogs

and Other Amphibians

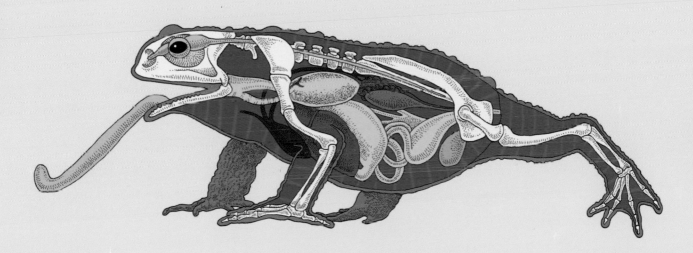

David West

WINDMILL
BOOKS

Published in 2018 by **Windmill Books**,
an imprint of Rosen Publishing
29 East 21st Street, New York, NY 10010

Designed and illustrated *by* David West

CATALOGING-IN-PUBLICATION DATA
Names: West, David.
Title: Frogs and other amphibians / David West.
Description: New York : Windmill Books, 2018. | Series: Inside animals | Includes index.
Identifiers: ISBN 9781508194279 (pbk.) | ISBN 9781508193937 (library bound) |
ISBN 9781508194330 (6 pack)
Subjects: LCSH: Frogs–Juvenile literature. | Amphibians–Juvenile literature.
Classification: LCC QL640.7 W47 2018 | DDC 597.8'03–dc23

Manufactured in China
CPSIA Compliance Information: Batch BW18WM: For Further Information contact Rosen Publishing, New York, New York at 1-800-237-9932

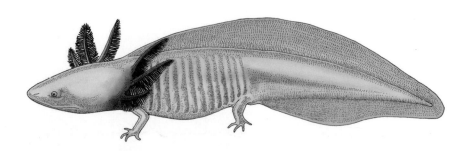

Contents

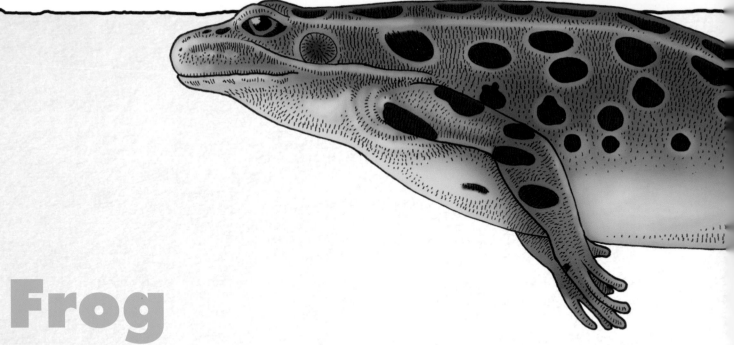

Frog

Like most amphibians, most frogs hatch from an egg as a tadpole with a tail and gills to breathe in water. They gradually change as they get older, losing their tail and developing lungs. As adults, frogs can live on land and breathe air. They must return to water to lay eggs. Like other amphibians, oxygen can pass through their moist skin. This allows them to remain underwater for long periods of time.

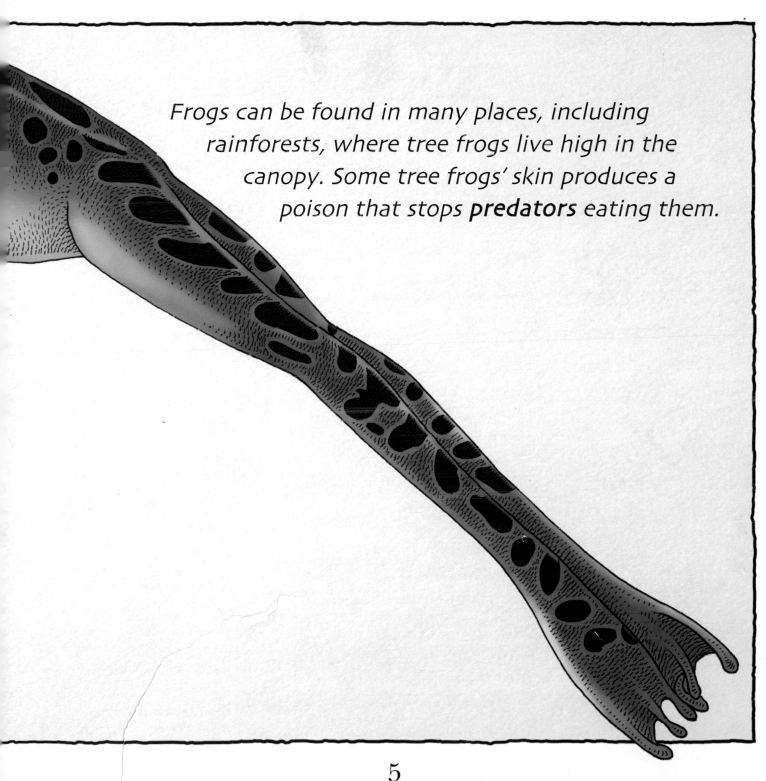

Frogs can be found in many places, including rainforests, where tree frogs live high in the canopy. Some tree frogs' skin produces a poison that stops **predators** eating them.

Inside a **Frog**

Skeleton

Muscles

Frogs have long leg bones and powerful muscles. Some frogs can jump 50 times their body length!

Eggs

Most frogs lay eggs, sometimes up to 4,000 at one time. Large numbers of eggs are called frogspawn.

Kidney

Cloaca

Webbed feet

Frogs' feet have skin between the toes called webbing. It helps them to swim.

Bladder

Intestines

Digestion continues in the intestines. Waste is ejected through a single opening called a cloaca

Skin
The skin of frogs and other amphibians is moist and very thin. This allows it to transfer oxygen to its body while it is underwater.

Brain

Ear

Tongue
Frogs catch **prey** on their long, sticky tongues.

Liver

Lung

Heart
Amphibians' hearts have only three chambers, unlike the hearts of mammals and birds, which have four chambers.

Stomach
Prey such as insects (especially flies), snails, slugs, and worms are digested in the stomach.

Toad

Toads are like frogs with dry, warty, leathery skin and short legs. **Glands** in the skin produce a liquid that keeps predators away. Toads live on land but always return to the same pond to lay eggs. They are nocturnal, which means they are active at night. Toads walk rather than hopping like frogs.

Toads can live in much drier places than frogs. They spend the nights hunting for slugs, spiders, and insects.

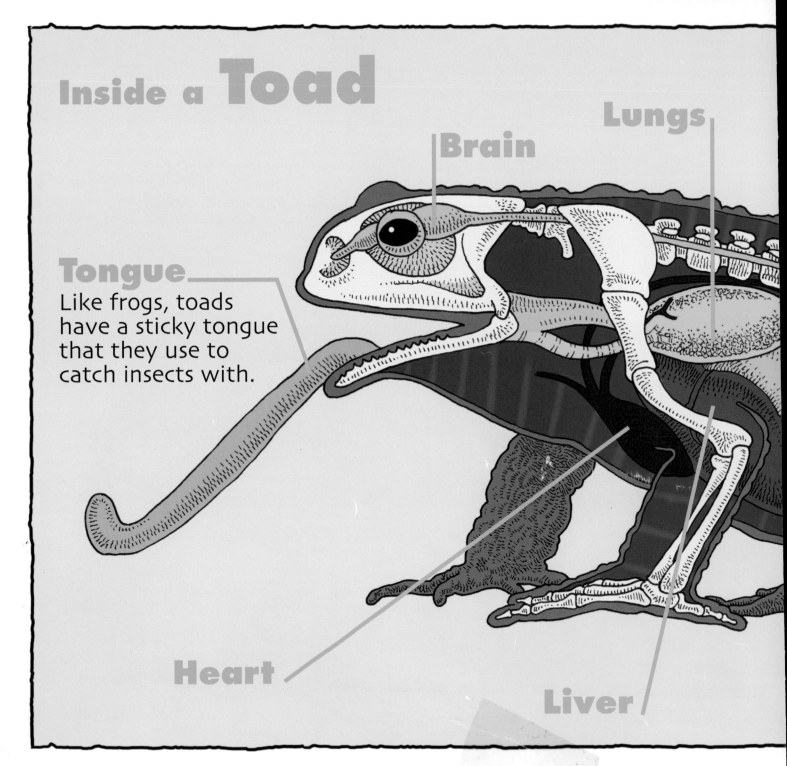

Inside a **Toad**

Brain

Lungs

Tongue

Like frogs, toads have a sticky tongue that they use to catch insects with.

Heart

Liver

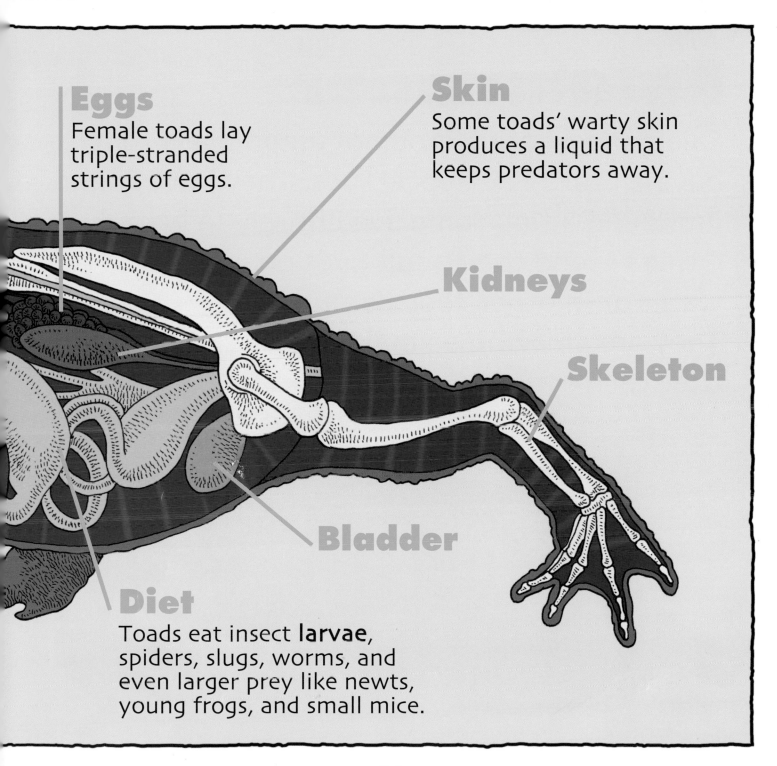

Eggs
Female toads lay triple-stranded strings of eggs.

Skin
Some toads' warty skin produces a liquid that keeps predators away.

Kidneys

Skeleton

Bladder

Diet
Toads eat insect **larvae**, spiders, slugs, worms, and even larger prey like newts, young frogs, and small mice.

Salamander

Salamanders are a group of amphibians that have a lizard-like appearance. They have four limbs and a tail. Some live entirely in water. Others spend their adult lives on land near water or in other cool, damp places. They are amazing animals since they can regrow lost limbs.

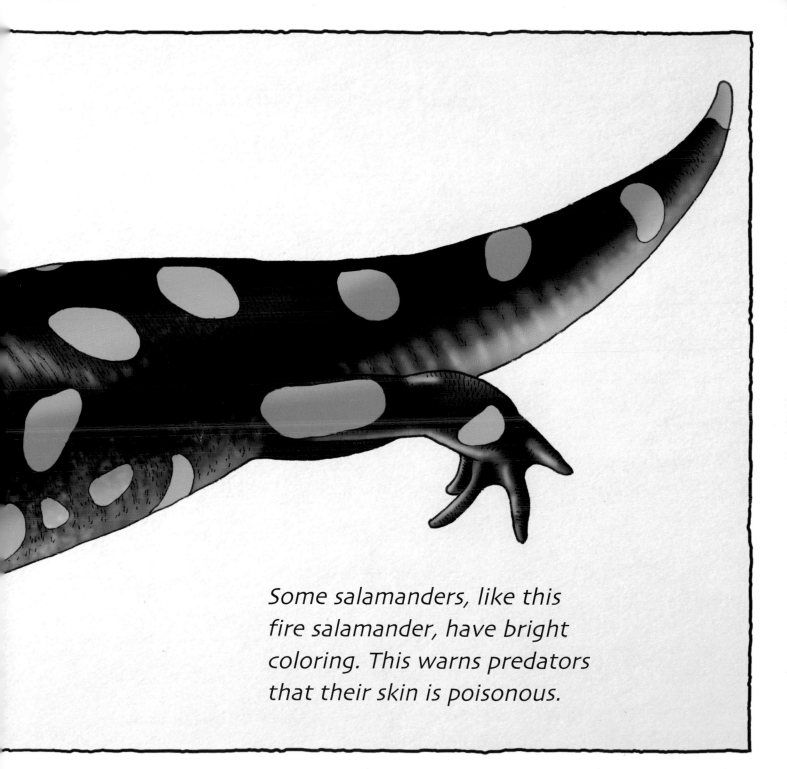

Some salamanders, like this fire salamander, have bright coloring. This warns predators that their skin is poisonous.

Inside a **Salamander**

Brain

Lungs
Lung size varies in different types of salamanders. Some have no lungs at all.

Ovaries
Salamanders lay eggs in water.

Heart

Liver

Stomach
Salamanders eat anything they can catch, from flies and spiders to earthworms and beetle larvae.

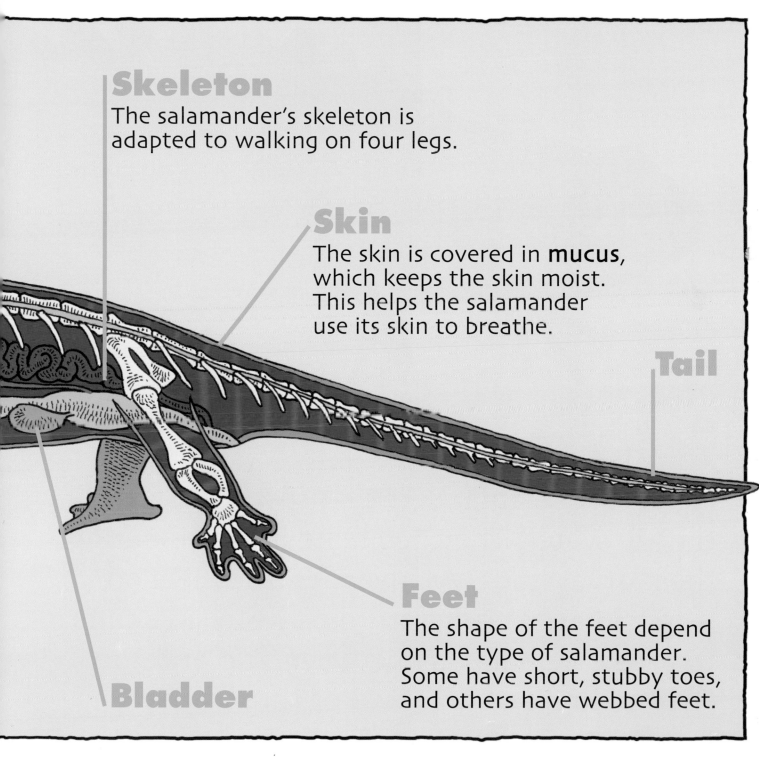

Skeleton

The salamander's skeleton is adapted to walking on four legs.

Skin

The skin is covered in **mucus**, which keeps the skin moist. This helps the salamander use its skin to breathe.

Tail

Feet

The shape of the feet depend on the type of salamander. Some have short, stubby toes, and others have webbed feet.

Bladder

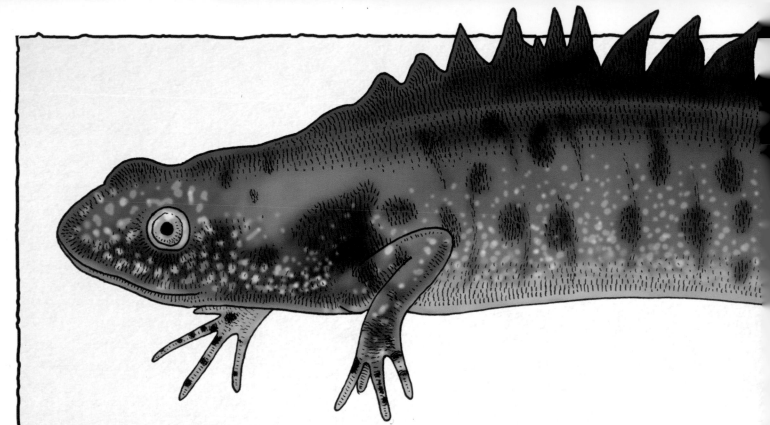

Newt

Newts are salamanders that spend a lot of time in water. They begin life in water during their larval stage. As juveniles, they live on land and eventually return to water as adults to breed. Females lay between 200 and 300 eggs at a rate of only two or three a day.

This great crested newt can grow up
to 6 inches (15 cm). It feeds on tadpoles,
worms, insects, and snails. During the winter,
it **hibernates** under logs and stones or in the mud
at the bottom of ponds.

Inside a Newt

Organs
Salamanders can regrow limbs, eyes, spinal cords, hearts, intestines, and upper and lower jaws.

Lungs

Skin
Like salamanders, many newts produce poisons from their skin as a defense against predators.

Brain

Heart

Stomach   **Liver**

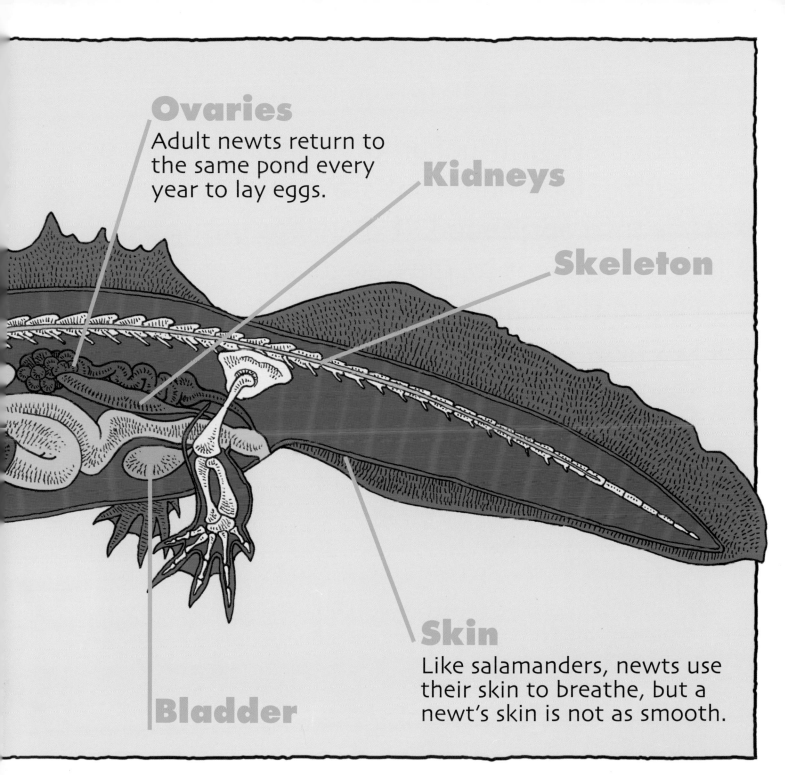

Ovaries
Adult newts return to the same pond every year to lay eggs.

Kidneys

Skeleton

Skin
Like salamanders, newts use their skin to breathe, but a newt's skin is not as smooth.

Bladder

Axolotl

Axolotls are unusual amphibians. They are a type of salamander that stays in the larval stage into adulthood. It develops basic lungs but keeps its gills, so it is never able to leave the water. Axolotls live in lakes near Mexico City, Mexico.

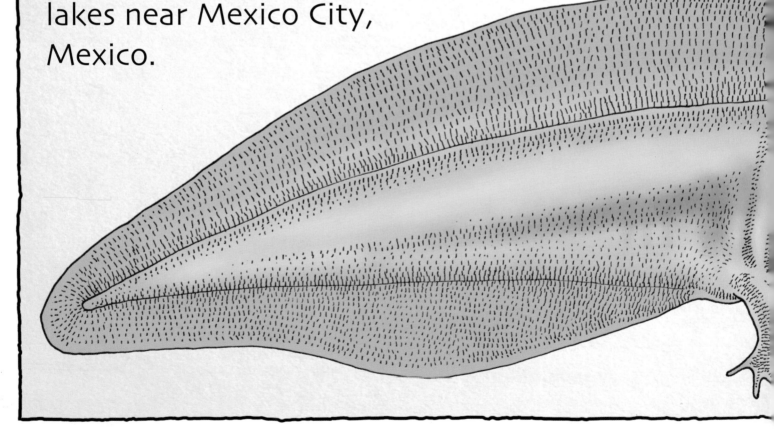

Axolotls can repair and regrow many parts
of their anatomy, such as limbs, and even
the less vital parts of their brains!

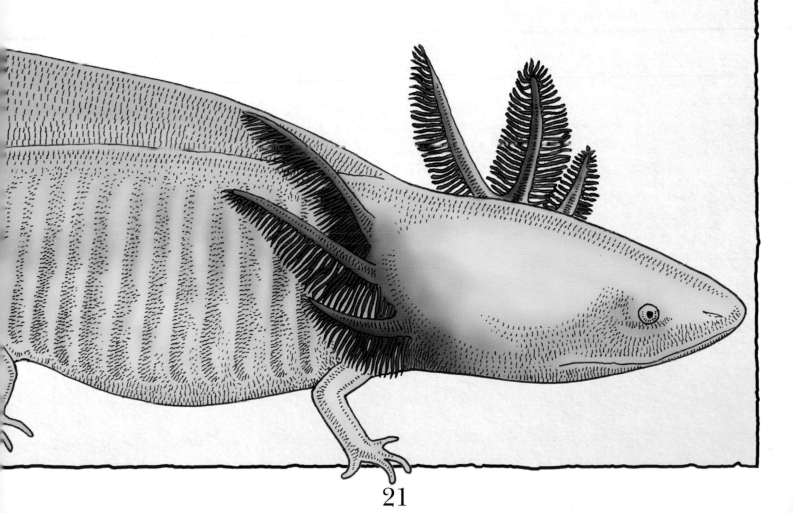

Inside an **Axolotl**

Fin

Skin

Some axolotls have white, transparent skin. Their skin has no coloration when they live in dark caves with no light.

Skeleton

Limbs

The axolotl has four limbs and is sometimes called "the walking fish," although it is an amphibian.

Lungs

The axolotl has both lungs and gills. It may gulp in air to help it breathe.

Gills

The axolotl has gills like a fish, but they are on the outside. Gills take the oxygen from the water and transfer it to its blood. This is how it breathes.

Brain

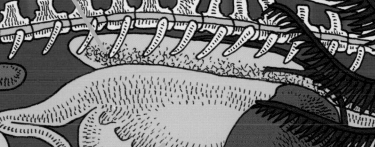

Stomach

The axolotl is **carnivorous**. It eats small prey, such as worms, insects, and fish, by sucking them into its stomach—just like a vacuum cleaner.

Heart

Liver

Glossary

carnivorous Feeding on animals.

gland An organ in an animal that produces chemical substances.

hibernate To spend winter in a sleeping state.

larvae The juvenile form of some animals, usually insects, before they change into adults.

mucus A slimy substance produced by some animals to protect their skin.

predator An animal that hunts and eats other animals.

prey An animal that is hunted and eaten by another animal.

Index